The Million Dollar Producer

My Journey from the Cotton Field to the Capital

By

Nancy E. Johnson

The Million Dollar Producer: My Journey the Cotton Field to the Capital
Copyright © 2019 by Nancy E. Johnson

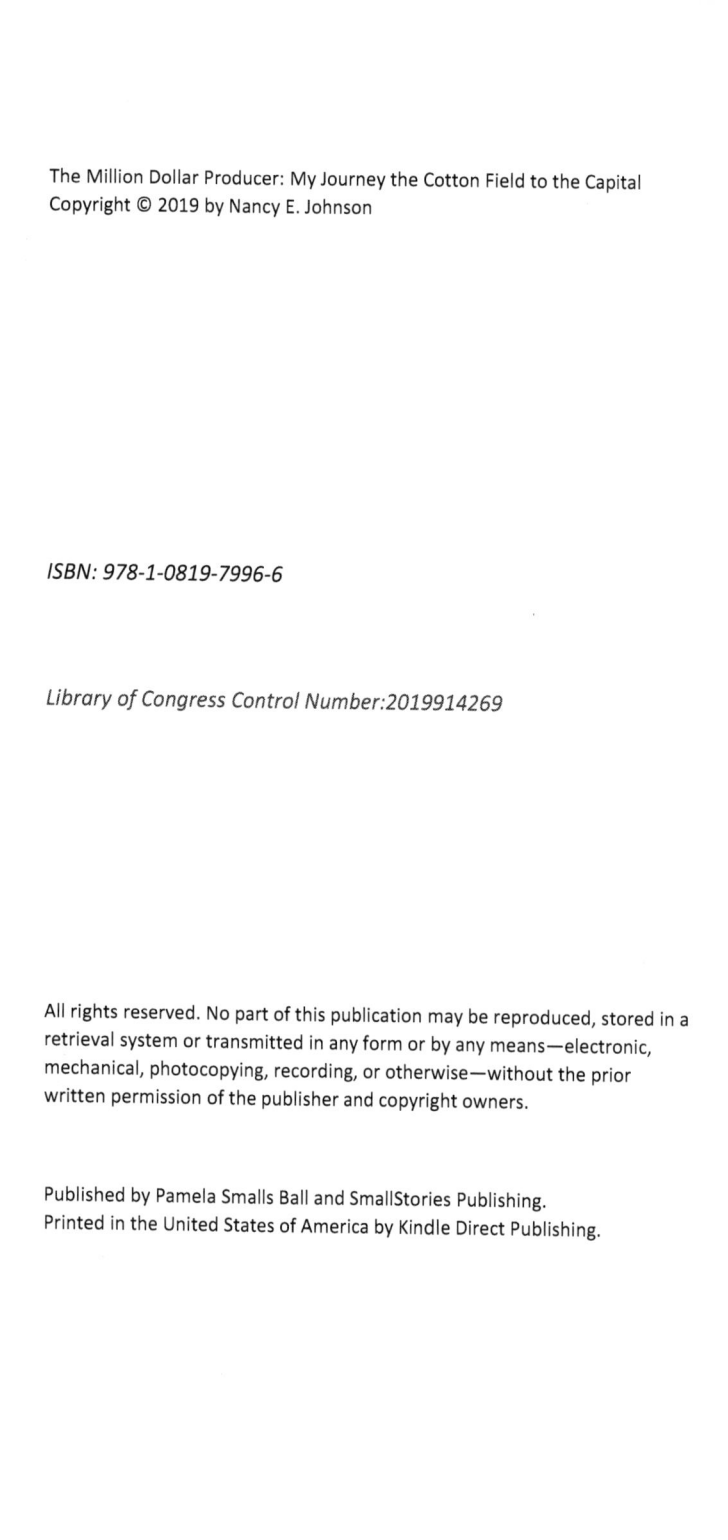

ISBN: 978-1-0819-7996-6

Library of Congress Control Number:2019914269

All rights reserved. No part of this publication may be reproduced, stored in a retrieval system or transmitted in any form or by any means—electronic, mechanical, photocopying, recording, or otherwise—without the prior written permission of the publisher and copyright owners.

Published by Pamela Smalls Ball and SmallStories Publishing.
Printed in the United States of America by Kindle Direct Publishing.

Table of Contents

Prayer	Page xii
Acknowledgements	Page ix
Introduction	Page 1
Part 1: From the Cotton Field	Page 7
Born with No Silver Spoon	Page 9
There's No Place Like Your Hometown	Page 13
The Baby in a Bag	Page 17
Blessed in the City...Blessed in the Field	Page 23
The Party Line	Page 29
My Moments of Recognition	Page 31
Mama Hen	Page 37
Raise Your Hand If You Want It	Page 43
Window Shopping	Page 47
Not on Sundays	Page 51
Downtown on Saturdays	Page 53
Taking Company	Page 57
Becoming Who I Was Supposed To Be	Page 61
Part 2: In the City	Page 65
Leaving South...Headed North	Page 67
My First Job	Page 71
Northern Exposure Ended	Page 77
In the Middle of It	Page 81

Balancing Act—Just the Two of Us	Page 85
Budgeting	Page 89
Southern Exposure in the Workplace	Page 91
They Pushed Me Too Far	Page 97
My Breaking Point	Page 103
It Had My Name on It	Page 107
Part 3: To the Capital	Page 109
A Leap of Faith	Page 111
One Billboard at a Time	Page 115
Radio Marketing	Page 121
The Glory Days	Page 127
Client Appreciation	Page 133
The Mid-East Experience	Page 137
Recession – Regroup – Rebound - Recover	Page 141
Speak Over Yourself	Page 151
When the Glory Comes: Real Estate Niche	Page 161
A Big Leap of Faith	Page 169
Paradise Was Part of The Journey	Page 173
The People on My Journey	Page 175
The No Excuse Zone	Page 185
Conclusion	Page 189
About the Author	Page 195

~ Prayer ~

Lord, you have been better than good to me! You have allowed me to climb some mountains that my small mind could not even conceive. I've been in some places, blazed some trails, broken many records, had lots of fun, and been more successful than I could have ever dreamed possible.

All my life experiences come down to simply being born to live in purpose. Thank you, Lord, for my journey from the cotton field to the capital. You planted me in the capital city in the right season for me and my family. My journey made me appreciate what could be, and what could not have been. I wouldn't trade it for anything. Life's journey is a teacher. Thank you, Lord, for the journey. Amen.

~ Acknowledgements ~

I have so many folks to thank in this book. There is a village of people behind my success in life. It is hard to name them all. For most, a thank you is not enough. All I can do is acknowledge that all of you have made a difference in my life.

I must give honor to God, who is truly the head of my life. He has kept me on the potter's wheel, molding, making, and refining me for such a time as this. He's been so good to me.

I first would like to thank my loving and supportive husband of 51 years, Ronnie. This book is your story just as much as it is mine. To my son Ronald, you are so much a part of the journey, and I love you dearly. To my daughter Tiffany, and my son-in-law Anton, you were my inspiration, head cheerleaders, toughest critics and coaches. I thank you two for pushing me to complete this book. To my grandchildren, Ronnie, Ashley and Damarion, this is but a part of the legacy I hope to leave with you about my journey. My desire is to be the example and leave a lasting legacy for you all, and for my great-grandchildren too.

I want to give special thanks to by birth mother, Annie Fulton Chandler, my second mama, Virginia "Aunt Honey" Fulton, Aunt Mary Houston better known as Aunt "Daughter", Aunt Ossie Mae better known as Aunt "Shug", Big Mama Laura Mullins, Uncle Elliott Fulton, and Uncle Willie James "C.J." and Aunt Francina Fulton. Thank you to my sisters and brothers, Ronnie, Sandra, Danny, Darryl, Donna, Vicky, Monica, Anna, Walter, Brenda, Linda and Michael who is deceased.

I also want to thank the Tisdale siblings who welcomed me into their family.

To my in-laws in the Johnson Family, my cousins, nieces, nephews, friends, there are too many of you to name, but know that you all have played a role in my life's story.

Some people are blessed to know their grandparents, and though I have not ever had that privilege, I have been tremendously blessed, and can surely testify that a village of relatives helped raised me.

It is because of you that I am who I am today. From sharing your homes, feeding me, clothing me, and encouraging me up to the present day, you all raised me. You've loved me from a four-walled house in the middle of a cotton field with an outhouse and no indoor plumbing, to a dusty dirty road called Sandridge, and all the way to the capital city of Columbia, South Carolina. Thank you.

I would also like to thank my real estate team and the many clients and past customers I have helped over the years. I am grateful for my church family, my coach Angela Patterson Carr, my mentor and coach Nicola Smith Jackson, and my publisher Pamela Smalls Ball.

Finally, to my readers, I would like to thank you for your willingness to read about how a country girl from one of the poorest counties in South Carolina made her way from what some may consider the bottom, all the way to the top in the in real estate. My prayer is that by the end of this book, my journey will motivate you to believe that no matter what your circumstances are, you can achieve anything you put your mind to, with hard work, dedication and prayer.

Introduction

There are some that would say that I am one of the most successful African American women ever to sell real estate in South Carolina. I would not ever try to make that point. I will say that I have been abundantly blessed in my real estate career. I have sold more than 2,300 homes totaling more than $40 million. I have achieved accolades that very few have accomplished. It is a fact…I have become a Million Dollar Producer. However, most people don't know my story. This book is my story.

I grew up in one of the poorest counties in South Carolina. I lived in a house that had four walls, no indoor plumbing, and an outhouse. I also grew up picking cotton and tobacco to earn money. Statistically speaking, most people that come from my circumstances would not be a Million Dollar Producer.

You might be wondering how I overcame my obstacles? Who or what helped me to make it through? Well, that is why I wrote this book.

In the following pages, I share my story and experiences growing up as a poor country girl from Kingstree, South Carolina. I didn't achieve this success by myself. It started with my faith in God, personal discipline, hard work and incredible life lessons that I learned from my extended family and mentors. One of the lessons I learned came from my cousin, Ernest Fulton. It was a lesson about the meaning and power of your name. Most people don't think about the significance or the meaning of their name. However, I recently learned something about my name that offers insight into who I am, and what I have become.

At my 65th birthday celebration, my cousin Ernest, whom I grew up with, and who was also like a brother to me, read a beautiful excerpt of what my name meant. The name "Nancy" was apparently a Hebrew girl's name, meaning "full of grace" and "one who has favor". My middle name "Elaine" is of French origin and stands for "shining light". Before this day, I did not know anything about my name, and I'm not sure that my mother knew the significance of naming me "Nancy Elaine" either. However, after you read this book and learn how my life has played out, you will see those meanings are divinely accurate to the calling God had on my life and I am grateful for it.

The book is written in short story format, all separately titled. Each one shares a meaningful experience, which speaks to the challenges I faced, my mindset and the values that I carry with me every day. As you read this book, I hope you will see how big God is, and what he can do in your life if you keep your faith in Him. However, this is not a religious book. It is my story. It speaks to the hardships I faced, the hurdles I have had to overcome, and how my faith kept me. The book also shares many of the business principles of hard work, taking risks, being a good person, and giving back to others, as keys to my success as a Million Dollar Producer.

In this book, you will learn, I had a difficult upbringing, but I don't make excuses. You will also learn that success in life begins with a vision of what you want for yourself. It's your mindset about your life and circumstances that will determine your outcome. I really believe that. You will also learn of the challenges and opportunities that corporate America gave to me, but how my destiny was not determined by a job. You will learn the importance of daring to be different and walking the road less traveled. That is what being an innovator all about. I share several experiences of how I stepped out on faith and charted new territory as a realtor in South Carolina. There are many other lessons that I share in the stories of this book.

Overall, I hope after you read it, you will be inspired to believe that you can overcome any adversity in your life. There is nothing too hard for God if you are willing to have faith, vision and a work ethic. It is with these principles, that my journey from the cotton fields to the capital city was made possible. I believe your story can be made possible too.

PART 1

From the Cotton Field

~ Born with No Silver Spoon ~

My young life was far from that of being born with a silver spoon in my mouth. I was the first born of twelve children. My mom, Annie Mae, was 17 years old and single, living in one of the poorest counties in the state of South Carolina, Williamsburg County. We lived in the country, down a dirt road, and didn't have much of anything.

Times were hard. Not just hard, but extremely hard. Now that I am reflecting, there are a few observations that would definitely qualify us as a dysfunctional family.

I was born to a teenage mother. My mother was living at home with her three sisters, a brother, and a very elderly father. My mom's sisters were Ossie Mae, Eliza Virginia and Mary Ellen. They all had nicknames that we called them by. Ossie Mae went by Shug, short for Sugar. Eliza Virginia was called Honey and Mary Ellen was the baby, we called her Daughter. My uncle's name was Willie James, but we called him C.J. My mother's nickname was Sweetie.

Sweetie could barely remember her mother, who died when she was five years old. After her mother died, Sweetie and her siblings were raised solely by their father, Sampson. When I was nearly, two years old, Sampson died. My Uncle C.J. lived with them on the farm to help make ends meet until he married at the age of 20.

Needless to say, there was no father figure in my life. I have never been in the presence of both of my parents at the same time…ever. I've only seen my father maybe three or four times in my entire life. To paraphrase the legendary singing group, The

Temptations, my father was a rolling stone. I was told my mother and another young lady were both pregnant at the same time, which makes sense, since my half-brother and I are about four months apart in age. It was strange for me growing up not having a relationship with my biological father. Yet I had a good relationship with his wife, Mildred Tisdale. I have also never met my mother's parents, nor my father's parents. I have only heard stories of my Grandpa Sampson, and seen a few photos but unfortunately, I have never even seen photos of the other three grandparents.

~ There's No Place Like Your Hometown ~

I grew up in Kingstree; a small town in Williamsburg County, South Carolina. As small as Kingstree was, the town was divided into several small communities. Everyone growing up there attended the same schools: W. M. Anderson Elementary and Tomlinson Jr. High School. My community, called Sandridge, was approximately five miles from Main Street where everyone shopped. If you lived a few miles North, South, East, or West of Main Street, then we said you lived up the track, over the river, in Rock town, in Nelson Field, or Crosstown. Every tribe had a claim to fame, and they all stuck together.

Everybody who was anybody came to town once a week. It was the social meeting place where we did our own version of networking. Downtown basically consisted of four streets, and we'd literally walk corner to corner for about four to five hours, meeting and greeting the same local faces.

Although Kingstree was small, we had many stores to get the things we needed. There was a Roses, a Five-and-Dime store, Drucker's Pharmacy, Dubins, Silvermans, Belk's, Cosmo, C. Tucker, Cato's, B. C. Moore's, Tomlinson Grocery, A & P Grocery, and Red & White Grocery. Whenever you forgot something downtown, you could get it at Miles Corner Store. We also managed to have a few black-owned businesses, like Speights Barbershop, Lawson's, McClam Shoe Repair, Burgess Barbershop, several hair salons and several dry cleaners too. And of course, there was Mr. Sammie Fulmore, who owned a soul food restaurant. You could always count on a delicious, hot, fried fish sandwich from his hole-in-the-wall joint.

No rural country town was complete without a juke joint and a piccolo for some good old soul music, and a good slow drag song. Wards Club, located up the track, was the main weekend hangout for this kind of soulful entertainment.

~ The Baby in a Bag ~

With all of the networking, socializing, and partying, there was definitely some baby-making going on in those cotton fields. Between the women cooking hot home-cooked meals on cast-iron stoves, doing chores, and working in the fields, they managed to have plenty of babies as well. Williamsburg County was known for having large families. Very few children could have the luxury of saying that they were an only child. The largest family I can recall was a family with 21 children! In my husband, Ronnie Johnson's family, he was the 12th of 13 children. I am from a family of 12 children.

From the 1940's to the 1960's, most babies in the county were delivered by midwives. An expectant mother would work up until her delivery time, and then someone would summon a midwife, or a woman skilled in the art of delivering children. This woman would carry a large black tote bag, filled with her medical equipment, and homeopathic medicine for both baby and mother.

When the midwife arrived at the home, she was prepared to assist the laboring mother and deliver the baby. Sometimes it took two to three days before the new arrival was born. The other children in the family were kept as far away as possible from the delivery site. Oftentimes, the other children were sent to stay at a neighbor's home during the delivery process. Pregnancy and delivery were rarely discussed. Most children just thought their mama got fat, and then Miss Laura (a local midwife) showed up and brought the baby. They viewed midwives as the "baby mailman", who came to deliver a package, which was in her big black tote bag. Children would say, "Oh! Here comes Miss Laura bringing the baby in the black bag!"

It was very rare for a baby to be delivered in a hospital. Most people did not have insurance coverage, or money to pay for the hospital stay. Midwives charged between $125 and $250 to help deliver children into this world.

Having a baby in a rural community created other challenges. For example, the inaccessibility to the county records office meant that simple clerical mistakes were often made on birth records. To this day, there are many adults that were birthed by midwives in small towns like Kingstree, who have challenges providing their accurate birth records. This topic often comes up when they try to get a copy of their birth certificate or verify the correct spelling of their names. There were very few cars and telephones in homes back then. It was difficult for the midwives to report a birth to the health department in a timely fashion. Therefore, the recording of information, such as birth records, was usually hit or miss. Oftentimes, the midwife did not get the spelling of the name, or the actual date of birth correct. They were also delivering a lot of babies around the same time, which also added to the confusion. To the best of their recollection, a child could have been born during tobacco or cotton season, or the child could have been born during the same month as another child was born. At best, a child's birth date and name were the midwife's best guess. I know of instances where people celebrated the wrong birth month and year until they were 65 years old and applying for Social Security. I salute the midwives of the olden days, for these pseudo-doctors did a great service for so many and received so little in return. It is hard to imagine

receiving only $125 to deliver a baby?

~ Blessed in the City...Blessed in the Field ~

I have to admit, I am very competitive, and always have been. I have vivid memories of seeing if I could jump to the other side of a ditch first, finish a spelling test first, and clean the house before my mom and my aunt had to tell me to do it. If it was hard work, I put my heart into it. Hard work was a given where I came from.

We never owned a farm, but I had a real appreciation for people who worked on them day in and day out. Growing up, my mom and her sisters never had a garden, much less a farm, so working in someone else's field was something they had to do to earn money. I never really saw my mom or her sisters working on the farm but working in someone's field is what I wanted to do to earn money too. Honestly, I chose to work and help my friends on the farm sometimes, even when there was no money to be paid. I just thought it was the neighborly thing to do to lend a hand.

It's funny at the age of seven or eight years old, I used to hear the word "sharecrop" and think, "I don't see them sharing the work in the fields!" Then I would be reminded that we didn't own much. We lived in a four-walled house in the middle of a cotton field. The house didn't have indoor plumbing. We didn't have a bathroom. We had an outhouse. We didn't own our house and we didn't own the field.

When it came to sharecropping, we were just the working hands for Mr. Motty Jacobs. Whenever crops were harvested, we got the seconds. But most families, whether headed by single females or not, were strong and resourceful. They knew how to make something out of nothing.

Mothers were blessed to make beautiful school clothes and Sunday clothes. Women didn't mind hollering across the field to a nearby neighbor and ask to borrow eggs, a cup of sugar, or even a dollar to put food on their tables. The struggle was real, and so were the hearts of the people in our community. It was a close-knit village. Not everyone had electricity, but we still had to figure out how to get our schoolwork done by the lamp light if necessary. We had to make do with what we had. We had no refrigerator, therefore fresh slaughtered meats were packaged with salt and hung in the smoke houses until the brutal cold weather arrived.

I still use and teach the principles that I learned early on in life. Particularly, the lessons I learned from my uncle, C.J., about sweet potatoes. C.J. was a farmer. He would plant and dig sweet potatoes and preserve the bulk of them using a process called banking potatoes. Farmers would dig a hole, lay down pine straw, bury the potatoes, and cover the hole with more pine straw and a lot of dirt. Then, when they needed a few potatoes, they would make a withdrawal. They had to be resourceful back then. Banking sweet potatoes is how we saved some for a rainy day. Most of the sweet potatoes survived and were used to make some of the most delicious pies.

We were raised to keep the little clothing we had cleaned, starched, pressed, and folded or placed on a hanger. Manners were very important, and not using them was unacceptable. *Yes Ma'am, Yes Sir, No Ma'am*, and *No Sir*, were the only responses allowed when responding to adults. *Yeah* and *No* were not an option.

When you know where you came from, and what you've been through, not only can you testify that God made a way out of no way, but you can appreciate the struggle, and be grateful for all your trials and tribulations. We all had hard times, but I've been blessed in the city, and blessed in the fields, and somehow, I made it through.

~ The Party Line ~

In the 1960's in Kingstree, the telephone lines were shared, but not the bill. Each family who was fortunate enough to own a telephone had to share the line with several other families. Yes, you paid your bill each month, but then you had to wait your turn to use the telephone in your own house.

Most neighbors played fair. However, some neighbors eavesdropped on other people's calls in order to announce that it was their time to use the shared party line. When that happened, you needed to hang up. When other people knew your business, your first thought was, "Did I talk about this on the telephone?" If you discovered that you did talk about it on the telephone, then you knew that *your* business was not *your* business anymore.

~ My Moments of Recognition ~

We all come to a point in our lives when we come to grips with who we are. For me, that moment happened when I was 10 or 11 years old. That is a pretty young age to have events shape your life and your destiny.

At that time, we lived in a one-bedroom apartment in Hallandale, Florida. Gulfstream Apartments was the name of the complex. This was where my mom, still a single mother, me, and three other children struggled. Our small, efficiency apartment was less than 600 square feet. It had a front door, a tiny kitchenette, and a makeshift bedroom, which was also our living room. There was one bathroom, and one closet inside the private bedroom. We had one full-sized bed and five occupants; my mom and four kids!

We moved to that apartment from Kingstree, where we had no indoor toilets, no television, no telephone, no electricity, and barely enough to eat. We felt like we had moved up in the world. I remember that the apartment complex mainly consisted of one-bedroom and two-bedroom apartments full of families from the Carolinas and Georgia. There were a lot of good, caring people who allowed others from back home in South Carolina to rent a room in their two-bedroom apartment. People were content with sleeping on sofas and rollaway beds.

This is the moment I vividly remember. On Saturday mornings, we would get a weekly knock at the door from a man. It was the rent man. He would come to collect the rent of $12. Oftentimes, we did not have the entire $12 to pay him. Our monthly rent was $48 to rent the apartment in Florida. Even those it was a small amount in today's dollars. It was very hard for us to come up with that amount in the 1960. My mom would often have to do a full day of work, and even half a day on Saturdays. She would clean toilets, iron, cook, and be a maid or housekeeper. When there was a knock at the door, she used to say, "Don't hide. Just give the Rent Man what I left him on the nightstand." But when there was nothing to give, I was told, "Don't open the door. Just tell him we'll try to have it next week."

At ten years old, I knew enough to ask why we were living under these conditions, and why is that man knocking on the door collecting rent every week. He wasn't just knocking on the door of apartment #5, our apartment. But he was knocking on all the doors in the complex. In my mind, I drew the conclusion that there were too many children, and not enough fathers to provide for them, and therefore, we have to pay to stay there. This was my moment.

It was at that moment that I made these declarations for my life:

- *When I grow up, I am not going to have a lot of children.*
- *I will never have to borrow clothes again, because I will have a lot of clothes.*
- *I will be married and have my own house with real floors. I will not have someone knocking on the door asking for money.*
- *One day, I am going to help my aunt get a bigger house.*
- *I want my own bedroom, and a place for my friends to spend the night.*

These were big dreams to state, but I was clear about what I wanted out of life. I never remember crying, or being sad and depressed about what others had, and what I didn't have, because I always declared that one day I would have the things I desired also.

~ Mama Hen ~

Have you ever heard the term *Mama Hen*? It refers to a person who assumes protective maternal responsibility for younger children. When my mother was working, I became Mama Hen. I was the Mama Hen for my five younger siblings. I was responsible and took a leadership role in caring for them. I had to clean the house, fix their lunches, and get them off to school. After they came home, I had to clean the house before my mother came home. Being the oldest was not all bad though. I learned a lot about self-preservation, setting the example, and making sure that there was enough to go around, before I got any of whatever we had. On some days, that wasn't much.

I was three years older than my brother, and he looked to me for leadership, and to help him with things. I helped him with his homework, made his lunch, and played games with him and our cousins, whom we lived with in our early years before we moved to Florida. Actually, we lived with them up until I was ten years old, and then my brother and I joined our mother in Florida.

You see, I was raised by a lot of people. I mean, I wasn't a foster child, but I didn't always have a permanent place to call home either. The Village always took a liking to me, and always encouraged me to do well. In my younger days, my mom had six children to raise. Almost all of them lived with different family members. The family members that I stayed with were single, with children of their own. Therefore, until I turned 13, the only father figure in my life was my uncle C.J. He was a mighty man of valor, full of character, and integrity. By this time, I had only met my biological father a few times in my life, prior to his death. My

Village included "Big Mama" Laura Mullins, my Aunt Daughter, Aunt Honey, and a host of other dear aunts and uncles who never gave up on me. Even when the journey was filled with cold nights and extremely hot, long days without heat or air conditioning, they cared for me. I was the only girl amongst six or seven boys, including brothers and cousins in the household. I cooked, cleaned, washed, and hung the clothes, and became very good at babysitting. Who am I kidding? I had no choice but to become good at babysitting!

Another thing that I learned, moving from the dirt roads of Kingstree, to the larger city of Hallandale, Florida, was how to budget. My mother would tell me to get some baby food, and something for sandwiches, and she would hand me four or five dollars. I would make a list, and my brother Ronnie and I would walk about one mile to the local grocery store. We had to tally the items as we went and select only the staples needed to provide for our family for two to three days at a time. We counted so accurately we rarely had to put anything back. At 11 and 8 years old, we got pretty good at finding bargains. Once we got our groceries, we would make our return trip home. We would proudly carry our brown paper bags filled with the goods we had purchased. In 1961, as best as I can remember, the list would consist of ten jars of baby food for one dollar, five loaves of bread for one dollar, and of course, peanut butter, jelly, corn flakes, and Kool-Aid somehow always made the list.

Being the oldest also meant that I had to be a supporter, an encourager, and a protector. I would also fight my younger siblings' battles for them. Although there were not many, being in a neighborhood where children played from around 10 a.m. until dark, there was bound to be a scuffle or two.

Yes, Gulf Stream Apartments #5 will forever and always be embedded in my memories. For me, that was the place where a single mom sent for some of the children she left behind and had them come and share a one-bedroom apartment with her. We saw a lot of hard times and worked to make ends meet. Times got a little easier once my mom got married and had the next six children. We eventually moved from the one-bedroom apartment, into a home in the nearby Carver Ranches community in West Hollywood, Florida. We had some good times in Florida, and being the oldest child helped to develop my character. I was empowered to do more, to know what I didn't want to know, and prepared to dream the impossible.

~ Raise Your Hand If You Want It ~

Do you know what it's like to be in uniform, or to wear the same clothes over and over again? Back in the day, little girls had panties and socks with the days of the week on them—Monday through Sunday. I've always wondered if the manufacturers were just trying to make sure we learned the days of the week.

In my case, I rotated my dresses, skirts, and blouses, mixing and matching what few pieces I had to build a colorful wardrobe. I always adored fashion and loved wearing bright, bold colors from head to toe. I loved sewing too.

Money was really scarce, and I remember a Catholic church located right in the center of our area of Sandridge Road. The priest and the nun either came from Boston, Massachusetts, or from somewhere in

New England. They were so kind and did plenty of mission work, by saving souls and helping the community.

One of their benevolent missions was to clothe the children. Tons of boxes of clothing were distributed every week. Sister Florence would stand in the front of the room, take the items out of the boxes, and showcase them from side-to-side. You'd have to raise your hand if you wanted the garment or shoes she showcased, and the lucky person selected would pay ten cents, and leave with a mighty good piece of clothing. Only ten cents! And although all of the items were not new, they were clean, most desirable, and greatly appreciated.

I must have had favor, or a desperate look in my eyes, because I wore many ten cent dresses and skirts with pride. I thank God for the journey, and the affordable prices, because fifty cents went a long way in my wardrobe. I could buy a whole outfit for twenty cents and have change to spare.

~ Window Shopping ~

At a young and tender age, I had already developed a taste for good fashion. Although I only had what you would call a pair of changing clothes, the Golden Rule was to always keep everything clean from my underclothes to my blouse. Whether it was a dress or a skirt, I had to wash them by hand a couple of times a week. Then I had to air-dry them, because there were no washers or dryers. I'll admit, I borrowed clothing items from my cousins, Gloria and Genevieve, who were very blessed to have nice dresses and shoes to wear to school and church. Gloria and Genevieve were Uncle C.J.'s daughters. I even learned how to sew in middle school, because I loved looking as good and as fashionable as possible. I could make my own bell-bottom pants, slacks, halter-tops, hip-hugger pants, and tent dresses. It was amazing what I could do with two yards of fabric!

When you're poor, or just not rich enough to shop where the good stuff is, you daydream and fantasize and think, "If only I could buy something there." Well, my daydreams and my night dreams were that as an adult, I would be shopping in a store called Silverman's Department Store on Main Street. It was the bourgeois store of our time. As a child or a teen, I had never even entered the

I was locked out then, but God opened the floodgates, and now it is my business to open doors!

doors. Why? Because they probably would have asked who I was, or why I was in the store. Personally, I never knew anyone like me who shopped there, but I would always window shop. It was a shame that by the time I could afford to shop at Silverman's, they had gone out of business.

Life is funny like that sometimes. I was locked out then, but God opened the floodgates, and now it is my business to open doors for others. As a realtor, I give keys to anyone who is ready to close a deal. I am now on the inside, handling my business, and I no longer have to just window shop.

~ Not on Sundays ~

Back in the day, you saved your best shoes, starched and ironed your best dress, blouse or pants for Sundays. Sundays were reverent, and not just for worship. There were certain things that you just did not do in the country on Sundays. There were no washing clothes, no ironing, no working in the fields, no dancing, no listening to blues music, no sewing, and no fishing. Of course, all stores were closed, including food stores. So, if you had work to do on the weekend, it was best to get it done on Saturday, or it would have to wait until the next week. Sunday's rules were strictly enforced.

At church, the members played a game of Round-Robin to see who would get the chance to prepare special meals for the preacher, who sometimes was visiting from another town. Feeding the preacher was a real privilege for country folks. The preacher always got the best of the best. Dinners consisted mostly of golden-brown skillet-fried chicken, garden fresh greens, fresh beans, potato salad, and lots of jelly-layered cakes and sweet potato pies.

~ Downtown on Saturdays ~

My hometown was in one of the poorest counties in the state, but we had lots of good times. Those were the good ole days for sure. Rural Williamsburg County had little to offer in the way of entertainment. We didn't grow up watching television. We actually didn't have one until I was in the fifth grade, and we had relocated to Florida. I cannot remember ever eating in a restaurant in Kingstree, except for the takeout soul food joint.

The small-town atmosphere wasn't a bad thing though. Role models were, in most cases, our parents, kinfolk, preachers and teachers. I can remember times when I missed school and rode on the back of a pickup truck to work on someone's farm, all the while hoping that none of my friends saw me on the drive back home.

Saturdays were special times though. The best social gatherings were either going to town on Saturday afternoons, or attending Sunday morning church services. We yearned for 3 p.m. to arrive, so we could get all dolled up, as we would call it, and walk around the four streets that made up our downtown area. This is when you could chat with your classmates and your boyfriend or girlfriend. This was our form of social networking, as we did not all have telephones, television, or internet back then. We passed the time walking and talking face-to-face with each other. Now-a-days, we ride to visit someone, and type and text messages to them. Times have surely changed.

> *This was our form of Social Networking, as we did not have telephones, television, or internet back then.*

Downtown was the hot spot to be on the weekends, and you either had to walk there or catch a ride. In my case, we would walk five to six miles from my community to downtown. Lord knows we got our exercise in. And that walk did not faze us either. We made sure to get downtown by any means necessary.

I think every small town, even the ones with two traffic lights, had a Woolworths, Roses, or a five-and-dime store. We knew how to make our small pocket change go a long way in the late fifties and early sixties.

~ Taking Company ~

Taking company, as we called it, was when a young lady around the age of 15 or 16 was allowed to have a boyfriend. In those days, the main times you would see someone that you had a crush on was at school, church, or downtown on Saturday afternoons. There were very few telephones! Some teens were fortunate enough to have the privilege of driving their parents' cars on Wednesday evenings, or on Sunday afternoons and evenings.

If you liked a boy, you would send a message through someone else, and most likely, the relationship would blossom during recess at school, or with him carrying your books after school. As the puppy love continued, he would ask if you could take company. Taking company was where he actually came to your house for two hours on Wednesday, and sat with you in the living room or on the porch. You looked forward to events like sock hops, dances, parades, and games, where you had an opportunity to smooch, slow drag, and sneak kisses.

But before you were allowed to take company, your parents had to know who your date's parents were. Many courtships back in those days ended in marriage. Now that I think of it, the majority of the married couples in my hometown were locals, and childhood sweethearts. For the guys with a special girlfriend, miles didn't matter. My high school sweetheart, Ronnie Johnson, who is now my husband of 51 years used to walk approximately five miles by foot, most times passing graveyards on an extremely dark country road, just to visit me. Did I mention that the road was unpaved? There was deep sand in some places, and sometimes it was muddy and cold in the winter, or muggy with mosquitos in the summer. That was true love if I do say so myself.

    Back then, parents didn't have to say much. Their actions spoke louder than their words. They would give you one pre-warning by saying, "Don't let me have to flip on the lights and say when it's time to come inside." We knew what the flipping of the lights meant, whether they spoke a word or not. While my boyfriend and I were on the porch, my Aunt Honey would either clear her throat, or call my name just once. I knew not to force her to have to call my name more than once. I also remember a stormy night when my boyfriend didn't have a ride home, and she got up out of bed, got dressed, and drove him down muddy, unpaved Sandridge Road to the other side of town. She wouldn't have done that for just anybody. Let's just say, he had favor with her.

~ *Becoming Who I Was Supposed to Be* ~

Coming from poverty and humble beginnings, you can quickly become labeled. It's up to you whether you allow your obstacles to set you back, or to set you up to appreciate, recognize, and shape your future. You get to choose, and yes, it is a choice. Reflecting on all the statistics and hardships in my past, things should have turned out very different. The odds were surely stacked up against me.

I was born to a 17-year-old single mother who had very little education, and no money. I was given away to a woman who could not have children, whom I stayed with for a while, until I was about eight to ten months old, and a God-fearing woman loaded her car, called the sheriff, and went house to house in a neighboring town to retrieve me. I had no father around for guidance and had only seen him a few times in my life before his death when I was in my late twenties. I moved from house to house, living with one relative or another, like a foster child. The blessing in this, was that I was placed in the care of loving people. I was raised in homes that had no water, indoor plumbing, or bathrooms until age ten.

Times were extremely challenging and tough, but I improvised. There was no alarm clock to wake me up for school, but I knew that I had to get up early enough to be the first one to take a sponge bath before everyone else woke up. In the winter, it was especially important to get up early, because I had to take the initiative to use a fat chip, a lighter, and kerosene, to light wood for a fire to warm things up.

Rural Williamsburg County was one of the poorest counties in the state. There wasn't even a welfare system. Compared to some of the surrounding counties and states, Williamsburg had some of the worst odds. Though times were rough, and we were poor, I was happy to wear hand-me-down clothing and shoes to school and work, because I knew that I was privileged to be able to even go to school.

I thank God for having angels watching over me. Although I was not brought up in a Christian home, I knew better, and attended church on my own. I excelled in school in my elementary years despite the difficulties I faced. I bought used school books, which we could barely afford, and scraped together twenty cents to buy reduced lunch.

Despite finishing in the top of my class, being selected for three out of eight senior superlatives, and being named the salutatorian of my class, I was not allowed to march at graduation, due to the strict rules of students having children out of wedlock. It didn't matter that I was smart, and that my boyfriend and I had plans to get married shortly after graduation...the Rule was the Rule. I was pregnant and could not walk across the stage at graduation. My boyfriend and I ended up getting married at the ages of 18 and 17, respectively. But more about that later. I wonder if they would reconsider in this day and age.

After graduation, my husband and I quickly devised a plan, and that plan was to go up North. Moving up North was our turning point. As my cousins and best friend went off to college, I was determined to work my way up the corporate ladder...all the way to the top!

PART 2

In the City

~ Leaving South…Headed North ~

On a cold February afternoon in 1968, I caught a Greyhound bus to Connecticut. This trip was kind of scary for a 17-year old that was six-months pregnant. I was trading in my dirt roads for snowy streets. I had never been to New England, but I had to go. My new husband had already gotten there before me and was waiting with an apartment just for the two of us.

I grabbed my seat on the bus, with one single suitcase and a brown paper bag packed with some good old fried chicken, bologna, chips, and candy. After all, it wasn't a ride that I had actually planned. I had only been north of Kingstree once with my cousins to Philadelphia. I was southern born and raised, and had only traveled between South Carolina and Hollywood, Florida, but never to New England. Until now.

It was an extremely long bus ride. We stopped in many small cities throughout the night, with people getting on and off, going here and there. I was so scared...too scared to sleep as we traveled during the night. I remember getting off the bus, and unbeknownst to me, the driver changed the sign on the front of the bus to "New Britain", which was another city past my stop in New Haven. With my small-town, little-traveled mindset, it might as well have said "Great Britain". I hesitated and began to ask several different people if it was the right bus, until I was comfortable that I was still going to end up in New Haven, Connecticut like my ticket said. Yes, I was a deep country girl.

Speaking of ticket, I must have looked at mine every half hour. I wondered, "What will this new place look like? What will it feel like?" I knew one thing...it was sure a long, long way from Kingstree.

I finally arrived at my new home, in the town of New Haven, where my husband already had a nice, cozy studio apartment ready for me and the expected arrival of our first-born child in the Spring.

~ My First Job ~

One year after arriving in New Haven, I was headed to my first real office job interview. I remember that day so vividly. We didn't have a car, so my only form of transportation was the city bus. At that time, it was a $0.20 token to get me to where I needed to go. I remember jumping on the city bus with that $0.20 token, wearing a nice, well-pressed gray dress, stockings, and heels. My hair was hard pressed with a hot comb. I also had a super nice bang swaying to the side. I was ready to smile, sit up with my back straight, with a confident stance, ready for my big interview.

By the time I arrived in downtown New Haven, I had to transfer buses. When I transferred buses, the skies opened up. There was rain and lightning all over the place. I quickly ran for cover with an old newspaper over my head that someone had left on the next seat. I had to protect my hairdo by any means necessary. My prayer was, "Lord, please don't let my hair puff up. Please don't let me be soaking wet."

I arrived at my stop and I was finally at my big interview. This ole country girl had journeyed all the way from small town Kingstree, to the big city for a chance to make it. I ran to the door, wet and scared, but hopeful. I needed this job, and I needed to redeem myself. I needed to prove that I could still be at the top of my class. I was an exceptional student from grade school through my senior year of high school. I was the salutatorian in the class of 1968. I was on the honor roll, co-editor of the yearbook, the head majorette, president of the drama club, voted best dancer in my high school, most congenial, and most popular. And yet, I wasn't allowed to march with my graduating class because I was pregnant. I knew that this was a challenge, and that this would make things harder, but remember, I was used to hard work, and I had prepared myself to work by any means necessary to make a way for myself. This job was the key to making a way for myself and my new family.

On this big day, the day of my interview, no rain, lightning, sleet, snow, or puffy hair was going to deter me from being a success. This interview was critical. It wasn't just about starting over, or being successful, but it was about redemption for me. Although I made a mistake, my attitude was, "I messed up, but I'm still a winner, and I will show this employer that I will be the best employee they ever had." I knew then that when I got the opportunity to sell myself in that interview, they would hire me, whether I had a diploma or not.

I put my game face on, walked in, took a deep breath, gathered myself, threw my makeshift newspaper umbrella in the trash, and put on a big smile. I looked at the receptionist and said, "I'm here for the interview."

With a shocked look on her face, the receptionist said, "We didn't think anybody would show up in this weather. It's nasty outside!"

She proceeded to say, "But since you're here, you can certainly take the typing test too."

Of course, I kept smiling, but inside, I knew I did not know how to type well.

She said, "Just try to do the best you can, and we will have a short conversation afterwards."

And from that day on, I was on the road to success. I was hired February 3, 1969 by a major insurance company. That day would be the first day of a 19-year career, which prepared me for the greatest life ever. Through the storm and the rain, I have no regrets, and I didn't complain. It was not easy, but it was worth it. To God be the glory!

~ *Northern Exposure Ended* ~

From February 3, 1969 through May 3, 1980, this country girl kept it moving. God just kept opening more and more doors for me. I had some hills to climb, but I made it. In the areas where I fell short, I made up for it with hard work and passion. Not only was work going well for me and my husband, but we also had two children now. We were finally old enough to get a car, and we had saved enough money to purchase three homes while interest rates were soaring.

> *God just kept opening more and more doors for me.*

My husband's job ended up relocating, and we decided to move back down south. We wanted to move to a new city that was bigger than the city where we were born and raised, so we chose to move to the capital city of Columbia, South Carolina. The plan was to see which one of us could get a job transfer the fastest, while the other looked for a new job.

Our move on May 23, 1980 was my second time ever seeing Columbia. The first trip was to interview and find a home. I came alone and within a week, had landed a job, and contracted to buy a home for our family. I guess I just had an eye for real estate and Jesus answered my many prayers.

Interest rates were on the rise, and our move was based on whomever got the job they interviewed for first. The bad news was that a company from Canada that my husband was waiting for, delayed their opening by six months. That door was closed. The real estate agent I was working with told me that I could apply for a loan to purchase our home. Although we had purchased a home previously in Connecticut, both had good credit and excellent income, our seasons had changed, and my husband was now unemployed. But, where there's a will, there's a way. I was introduced to an alternative method of financing called loan assumption, for people in a bind. So, we withdrew $16,000 from our bank account and signed on the dotted line to assume a loan. Sixteen thousand dollars was a lot of savings to part with at one time. We were in a new city, my husband had no job, and I had just taken a $5,000 pay cut to start at the bottom of the totem pole, having worked at Blue Cross Blue Shield of Connecticut for the last 11 years. We walked by faith and made the move.

~ In the Middle of It ~

After growing up in a predominantly black neighborhoods in Kingstree, Hallandale, and West Hollywood, the move North in 1968 landed us in a multi-cultural neighborhood. Italian, Jewish, White, and African-American people filled the streets of New Haven and West Haven, Connecticut. It was a true representation of the proverbial melting pot and was the total opposite of my birthplace in South Carolina.

On May 23, 1980, we rolled into Columbia, South Carolina, with the U-Haul packed to capacity. Funny thing, our realtor was a white female from Ohio, and she was really cool, and eager to work with me. My husband was still in New Haven, and not on the house hunting trip with me. She showed me homes in Northeast Columbia that were close to my new job. I didn't know anything about the city at this time, like which neighborhoods I should look at vs. which neighborhoods I should stay out of. We then purchased our first Columbia home.

As we settled in, we started to take notice, first of the children, and then the adults. Not many of them looked like us. In fact, there was only one other black family in a subdivision of over 150 homes in 1980. We were smack dab in the middle of it. A dentist lived to the left of us, the top OB/GYN behind us, a contractor to the right of us, and a professor and the owner of a real estate company directly across the street from us. This was totally unplanned. We didn't intentionally move into an all-white community, but it happened. It was a good location and a good move for us. Perhaps it was God's sign of things to come.

The children became fast friends, and usually played outside until dark. They mainly played in our yard, where there was a circular driveway and a basketball goal. Both of our children were athletic and tried out for both the school and recreation teams.

Though we just kind of landed in the Greengate neighborhood, we got very comfortable, and stayed there raising our family for 17 great years. We also purchased three or four properties over the years in this same area and flipped them for profit.

It's funny how life turns out. God's moves are better than our moves. His moves have purpose. I came all the way from a one-bedroom house in the middle of a cotton and tobacco field, to the capital city, living where I chose to live. We serve a mighty God and His word is true. He declared, "You are the head and not the tail." He will show you favor and bless you with more than you could ever think or dream.

~ Balancing Act—Just the Two of Us ~

Once we relocated to South Carolina and landed in Columbia, we had to gain our footing. Our two children were in elementary and middle school, and there were no parents, grandparents, sisters, brothers, nor in-laws living in this new city we called home, for us to depend on.

Our journey had begun in the country town of Kingstree, then New Haven, and now had transitioned to the capital city, Columbia, South Carolina. By that time, I had worked for Blue Cross Blue Shield in Connecticut for eleven years before I transferred to the Columbia location, where I worked for seven more years.

Marriage, being a mother, taking the children to their activities, keeping the house clean, cooking meals, and working full-time, required a lot of planning and family support, but somehow, we managed it all. On Saturdays, we always had something going on. There were trips to visit family in Kingstree, cookouts, children's games, and Ronnie also played softball on a couple of teams. Preparation for the week gave me an advantage and saved me a lot of time to do other things, like help with homework.

On Sundays, meals were prepared to last us through Thursday. I had a double oven, and I took full advantage of it. Sunday meals almost always consisted of fried chicken, rice, collard greens, and cornbread, or macaroni and cheese. A pot of stewed beef, meatloaf, and neck bones was the plan for the next few days. Mealtime was mostly just heating up already prepared meals, and not cooking new meals every single day. Corndogs, pot pies, and pizzas were fillers that the children could easily make on their own in-between meals.

~ Budgeting ~

Budgeting was a consistent and serious thing in our household. It was planned and executed every payday. When you come from a big family, where everybody is barely making it, and you can only rely on each other when things get tight, budgeting is essential to survival. I've always prided myself on saving money and reading about people who found ways to become successful and wealthy. I honestly didn't have a wealthy circle. Most of the young couples, or people in their twenties that I knew were raising children, still partying, working, or buying cars, and did not have the wealth-building mindset.

Thank God for a partner that trusted me with the finances and the responsibility to handle the day-to-day business for the family. We gathered around the table several times a year and budgeted three months ahead. It was our mindset that if we were ever going to have anything, then we would need to work hard and build our savings. Though we married young, we took our responsibilities very seriously. Balancing family, finances, and our future by budgeting, and owning several businesses worked for us, and allowed us to build multiple streams of income.

~ Southern Exposure in the Workplace ~

The transition into our new community was mild, compared to living in the middle of a cotton field, eating scraps at times, moving to Florida, then to Connecticut, then back down to a still racially-divided South Carolina. Race was still very much an issue, and the workforce was a challenge, even for the strong at heart. I took a $5,000 pay cut, just to get the only position available, or so I was told. It was intriguing, learning the "Good Ole Boy" system. It started with my first position.

My supervisor was on medical leave, so I interviewed with the vice-president of the department. I later learned that my interview with the vice-president created discord amongst the employees, who thought that I was there to replace the supervisor. That supervisor later returned to work with a hammer of vengeance, and with the thought that no three-piece, designer-suit wearing black girl was just going to come in and take her job.

As you can imagine, the blame game got hot and heavy in the capital city for me. Finally, after an unsigned performance review, and allegations of incompetency, my supervisor and I had a faceoff, where she admitted that she was wrong, and that she felt threatened, and thought that I was trying to show her up. I just kept thinking, "Can we all just work together?" The answer was no. We could not all just work together.

I later found out that two young black females in the department that I thought were my friends, had poisoned my supervisor's opinion of me. They had spread lies, drama, and hatred to the returning supervisor, and had stirred all of this up before the new supervisor and I had even had a chance to meet.

The best solution, short of a lawsuit, was to allow me to transfer to a different department for a fresh start. I agreed. After I transferred out of that department a floodgate of aggressive promotions started, and I continued to receive them for the next seven years. During that time, God sent me an angel by the name of Joy Youngblood Elliott, to help me navigate the rugged terrain of corporate America. She became my mentor. She supported me and gave me great advice and good direction. I followed her lead, and I was able to make it through.

In the 1980's, African-American women in the South were still not fully seen or recognized as leaders in the business community. When I arrived, there seemed to be many women working in the insurance industry, but there were no black managers and very few supervisors. Out of 2,000 total employees at Blue

Cross, there were only two black supervisors. I was one of the two. There was only one other African-American in leadership, a director. I thought to myself that this wasn't right. There were plenty of African-Americans working at Blue Cross, and I thought we should have more representation in leadership roles. I wanted a larger role, and to make more money, but I knew that it was going to be difficult to get an opportunity for promotion at Blue Cross.

Thoughts of leaving Blue Cross were bleak and just a notion. I didn't have a real plan. I applied at BellSouth, because they had a reputation for paying well. However, you had to take an entry exam. They claimed the exam was to ensure you were capable of doing the jobs they offered. However, most never knew if they were capable or not. You would be tested, but they didn't have to disclose to you what score you made on the test.

A test, but no test scores meant that you wouldn't know if you passed or failed. It was a shot in the dark. So, I took the entry exam, but was denied the position. I had every reason to believe that I aced the test, but the letter I received from BellSouth said that I had failed. I didn't, and still don't believe that I failed. However, because I didn't get the position, I still had to stay at Blue Cross. I just could not afford to quit and go back to school. We needed the income now. So, I had to shift my thinking. The impossible was now going to have to become the possible, because I refused to give up, give in, or settle for less in the South, no matter what others did.

> *The impossible was now going to have to become the possible...*

I dug my heels in and kept praying and working my way in and out of various positions within Blue Cross and Blue Shield. I eventually earned a position as a manager in the claims department. I thank God for my mentor, Joy, or I may have really hurt somebody back then. It was hard being a black woman in corporate America. The fight was still in me, whether I worked in the North, or deep in the South.

~ They Pushed Me Too Far ~

I was forced into the best opportunity of my life. What was meant to destroy me, or press me, actually helped me to build an extraordinary future. I always put my heart and soul into every assignment. It didn't matter what was tossed my way. I have always bought into the mindset of doing twice as much to get half as far. I knew that life wasn't always designed to be fair.

There were very few surprises in the corporate world, especially from the 1960's to the 1980's, when I worked my way up the corporate ladder. I felt very blessed to be a manager in one of the largest insurance firms in America. I entered the workforce with both feet solidly planted on the ground and rose to the top. File clerk...no problem. Special audit clerk...no problem. Technical support and customer service representative...I can master it. Supervisor, manager...you bet I can do it. The whole time, I'd been waiting for the chance to advance to upper management. I was labeled as a "Firestarter" and a "Trailblazer". I moved around a lot in my 19 years of service. I learned a lot and gave even more.

I prayed for the promotion of all promotions, or something that I would deem my big break. That moment came, and it was a surprise. Let me explain why.

Most of my work was in the claims area. Most of the managers were female, without college degrees, and most of them were five to ten years older than me. One of the directors had even become a very supportive and encouraging mentor to me. However, there was one thing that stood out in many of the long meetings.

You couldn't miss the fact that I was the only African American out of all the department heads.

The week had ended well, and our numbers were up. The two junior vice-presidents and directors, which were women, and two managers, including myself, were celebrating our success. Generally, we would talk about our success, and the following week's meeting. I expected it to be a good meeting. However, it was at the next weekly meeting where things hit the fan, and they pushed me way too far.

Here's what they announced:

"Good news! You all will get a small token of appreciation for your success last week. Also, we will eliminate a vice-president position, and combine the departments, and Nancy will be responsible for 16 new employees. We will promote another manager to director, but we cannot promote any manager that does not have a college degree. We do have other employees that have been grandfathered in, when degrees were not required, but no one else will be promoted without a college degree."

Here's what I heard:

"Good news! You all get a small token of appreciation for your success last week. We will eliminate a vice-president position. We will promote one manager, which will not be Nancy. And now Nancy will be responsible for 16 new employees. We will increase her staff and increase her new team's production expectations. We know that we could have promoted Nancy, but she doesn't have a degree. And although we made the exceptions before, we will not do so for Nancy."

What was said rang loudly in my ears, at an extremely high volume of discrimination.

Here's how I reacted:

I listened and stared with a poker face. I had felt it coming. The only other manager in the room was promoted to director, and I was told I deserved it, but I didn't have a degree.

~ My Breaking Point ~

This was the moment of awakening. From this point forward, I was a pit bull, breathing and sinking my teeth in at the same time. I knew that I needed to work just hard enough to keep my job. Before this, I had nearly perfect attendance, and loved showing up to work. However, my remaining days of service lacked passion. I had to remind myself who I was, and what my purpose was. I was being pushed to the brink and didn't know how to turn back.

I called a meeting with my boss, and her boss, and presented them with a written ultimatum. It read, *"I just received an exceptional performance review and was assigned more employees. Let the record show that if I suffer any physical, mental, or emotional strain as a result of this unfair practice, that you will be held totally responsible."* Needless to say, the meeting went poorly.

I was asked to meet with the Equal Opportunity Director and was asked to please retract my letter. Of course, I refused. The next day, I was so emotionally spent, that my doctor ordered a heart monitor, and six weeks off from work. When I returned six weeks later, I was tossed into solitary confinement, meaning I put into an office by myself, with a chair, a desk, and an empty bookcase. I felt isolated and oppressed. However, not defined by my circumstance, I was obsessed with finding my purpose. I knew this role at Blue Cross was a temporary holding place, and not my life's destiny.

I needed to figure out what I was meant to do. I began to think, "What can I do to earn an exceptional income while helping people?" Not getting the promotion I desired, and not settling for my bosses' explanations on why I didn't receive the promotion, caused me to pursue real estate. I figured, if I was going to work like a dog, then I was going to build my own doghouse, and make it the best doghouse possible. I didn't know it at the time, but their actions pushed me into the best profession ever. I saw then that even my bad works out for my good, and I thank God for the push out of my comfort zone.

I gave the insurance industry the best I had for 19 long years, and then it was time for a change. I discovered that a J.O.B. (**J**ust **O**ver **B**roke) could never pay me what I was actually worth. Degree or not, I had my mind set on making a lot more than what any JOB offered. I needed a different level of compensation and moving from the comfort of a W-2 employee to the unfamiliarity of a 1099 contractor was my ticket to financial comfort. I had to take the plunge. In hindsight, the trip, and the time spent on the journey was necessary. He was preparing me for a greater work.

~ It Had My Name on It ~

I must admit, transitioning out of my job was a process. The first and hardest step for me was deciding to let go. Getting out of my comfort zone, and leaving a steady job was hard. My second step was to grab hold of a

> *When you depend on a paycheck, it may be secure...but it is far from financial security.*

new business, a business where I would be solely responsible for whether I succeeded or failed. I started minding my own business. When you depend on a paycheck, it may be secure, and you know that you'll get it, but it is far from financial security. When I was in isolation, my mind was quickly asking and answering hard questions, one after the other. Questions like:

- *Do I need more income?*
- *Do I need to have a college degree to be successful?*
- *Are there any other job offers available for me?*
- *What am I good at?*
- *Can I make money doing what I'm good at?*
- *What can I do right now to have an unlimited source of income, without a formal education?*

All of these were important and thought-provoking questions, and I knew that I needed to answer these questions before I could move forward.

PART 3

To the Capital

~ A Leap of Faith ~

The transition from working for 19 years with the security of steady paycheck, to becoming an entrepreneur and working strictly off of commission, was not as tough as you might think. For me, it was more about what caused the breakup—19 years of being promoted, and then one day, you find out that your work cannot speak for itself, or promote you to the next level, all because you didn't have a degree.

I refused to settle, and I refused to be undersold. I made the decision to take off the guard rails, charge full speed ahead, and to be the best I could be while doing it. This left me with a burning desire to make real estate my get-out-of-jail free card, and my vehicle to roads less traveled by a young, black woman. The funny thing about the transition was that I never even thought that I wouldn't make it. When I look back today, I'm surprised at how far God has allowed me to succeed on my journey to opening doors for others.

As with all transitional or pivotal moments in my life, I had a Plan A, and a Plan B. But honestly, when I decided to make the transition, my mind, heart, body, and soul screamed, "You got this! This is your cup of tea!" I never thought it would not work. I just kept being surprised at how well it worked.

Some people tend to test the waters of real estate, by sticking their toes in to see how deep the waters are. I never tested the waters of real estate. I just jumped in with both feet. Once I got in the water, I thought, "Whoa! This feels good!" After that, I never looked back.

I vividly remember the days of on-the-job isolation, where I would use white index cards to write down my dreams and goals. I remembered writing "double my income and make a whopping $50,000 a year"! That was in 1985, and after quitting that job, I made $37,000 my first year, and that was only the beginning! The push and the decision to move on was the best thing I could have ever prayed for! Change can be good.

~ One Billboard at a Time ~

In business, you have to find what works, and then work it hard, fast, and furious. Columbia, the capital of South Carolina was a new home for us back in the early 1980's. It was a wonderful city to start a business in, but the major problem was that since I was the new girl in town, I did not have a sphere of influence. And in real estate, that is a must. You must build a list of everyone you know and start calling to see who is in the market to buy or sell real estate. We didn't have family, friends, a fraternity or sorority family, or military connections to prospect.

Since our children were heavily involved in sports, that helped us. We were able to meet and build rapport with other families at the park, or on the field. This was a slow process. Aside from those who knew me from work, or the small church we attended, I was an unknown newbie to the Columbia real estate market. I knew that if I was going to be successful, I would need to do more than just wait to meet people at the ball field, at work, or at church. So, I quickly assessed my environment and made some tough choices. I decided to beef up my marketing campaign and committed to spend more money to become a household name in the housing arena.

During the late 1980's, there were very few African-Americans on billboards, particularly in the south. And if you did see an African-American on a billboard, it was either a cigarette ad, or a hair product advertisement. There weren't any African American entrepreneurs or real estate agents on billboards. A light bulb went off in my head and I thought, "Do what you did as a young girl growing up in the country. Use what you got to get what you need."

My bright idea was to get innovative. It was time to take lemons and make lemonade. I felt that if I put up billboards in the right locations, surely, I would get noticed. There were two main reasons I believed this. First, I would be one of the few black faces on billboards, which would create a shock factor, and second, because no other realtor was advertising on billboards. Thousands of people saw my face, my business, and my phone number. When they saw me in public, they recognized my face. When I approached people about buying or selling houses, they would put two and two together. Even the newcomers paid attention to the billboards. If there was one thing I knew, it was that if someone was not in the market to buy a home, they would still remember a long time afterward that I was the realtor on the billboard, because it stood out. I stood out. I can testify that no one ever got me confused with another realtor because of my billboard. Many years after my billboards were taken down, people still say, "Hey, I remember you," or "I remember you and your daughter on the billboard."

> *This was one time where it paid to be the minority and not the majority.*

Billboards were so effective in those days, because no other realtors were really advertising on billboards except one other top-producing agent, who specifically marketed exclusive Million Dollar Homes. And there were definitely not any African-American women realtors who were on billboards. This was one time where it paid to be the minority, and not the majority. I became a well-known and trusted familiar face in many communities, especially the minority communities. I was known and recognized for my hard work, caring attitude, and professionalism.

Overall, I would say the decision to market my business on billboards established me as a pioneer and a trailblazer in the Columbia real estate market. I am still sipping on the residuals of some good ole country girl lemonade. I just love it when God's plan comes together.

~ Radio Marketing ~

I knew that billboard advertising only would not sustain my business, especially after others began to catch on and follow. Another valuable lesson I learned as a young country girl, was never to put all of your eggs in one basket. I knew I had to have a "Plan B".

In the late 1980s, newspaper ads worked great. We had no internet, no virtual tours, and there were very few model homes. My newspaper subscription was a delight. I could not wait for the weekly top producer announcements to come out. The community would get a feel for how your business was growing based on whether they saw you in the weekly Top Producer realtor section. Although I and many others enjoyed reading the newspaper, there were others that simply weren't going to read them. My thought was, *"If everyone isn't reading the business section, how do I get the word out about my business if they don't see my face in the newspaper?"*

This was when I decided to try radio advertising. I had to figure out what particular group of people would most likely be buying a home, and then I had to cater my marketing to that audience on the radio. I had lots of questions, such as:

- *What time do they listen to the radio?*
- *What station do they listen to?*
- *What would pique their interest to call me?*

Again, after much prayer, and with the wisdom and advice of a local Pastor and good friend, Josh Lorick, I decided to start advertising on a gospel radio station. Pastor Josh Lorick was a constant on the radio. He was a local preacher who also had a great radio voice. They called him, the "Golden Voice" radio announcer. After my conversation with Josh, I knew that gospel radio had a limited audience, because everyone didn't go to church and the station went off at 7pm at night. But I went with my gut.

I reached out to the only gospel station in town, which was also then an AM station with limited range. However, my decision to utilize the airways for marketing and getting my name out there, was the second-best thing next to sliced bread! It would turn out to work like a charm.

Radio advertising worked magic for my business for many years. In fact, the station owner followed-up with me after one year of advertising, which was around 1988-1989. I was utterly amazed when I saw that as a result of the radio ads, I had earned an additional $48,000 that year! The voice overs, personal ads, and of course, the client's live testimonials, were just what I needed to take off. My real estate business propelled to levels far beyond what I could have dreamed or expected.

I used Billboards and radio advertising to build my brand. They were the most powerful ammunition for me. They worked extremely well together. When I decided to advertise on billboards and gospel radio, I studied and prayed for just the right results. The blessings were exceedingly and abundantly more than I could ask for or think of, and I knew that God was the reason for it all.

All I could think about, was that I was just a little poor girl, who grew up in the small town of Kingstree, with no television, who had never even seen a billboard for the first 15 to 17 years of her life. But look at what God can do. Who would have imagined that years later, I would be seen on television, in newspapers, and on billboards, displaying my success in business? Some call it vision, but I always say, when the Lord knows your end from the very beginning, even the stars will line up for you. As hard as one might push, they would get smashed trying to close any door God opens for me. It won't work. He has the final say.

~ The Glory Days ~

The real estate deals were turning like hot cakes. I loved setting big goals. These were the years to shoot for the stars, and I did. This country girl said, "Yes, I can do this! I love to open doors!" In fact, my goal was to break some records, and become a millionaire by doing it. Around 2005, I decided to turn up the heat.

Business was booming, and there was enough for us to share. I decided again to become resourceful and use what I had access to. It was at that time that I officially created the Results Partners. With this move, I raised the bar by creating a real estate team. Teams were not a part of the Columbia, South Carolina market, except for a few husband and wife teams. Most agents preferred to fly solo. My vision for building a team came from my exposure of attending real estate conferences all over the U.S. I attended conferences in California, Las

Vegas, Florida, Colorado, and Texas. This exposure introduced me to new people, new places, and fresh ideas of how to grow and build a big business. I was excited and ready to try. It was time to expand, to leverage, and to enlarge my territory. Being the first person to do a thing has its share of rewards and challenges.

It was at this time that my bestie, my daughter Tiffany, had a dual role as my assistant and trusted business partner. We were known in the industry as the mother-daughter team. Our business soared from 1986 to 2004. But it was time for a shift. Since business was booming, I saw no reason why we shouldn't do the same.

When we formed our team, we were charting unknown territory with this team strategy. I strongly embraced the concept that we could accomplish more by leveraging our time. I could no longer fly solo, and be the only rainmaker, but I had to start sharing the success, the wealth, and the deals. Because the team concept was new, it was also very complicated, empowering, and disappointing at the same time. Author John Maxwell said it best, "Sometimes you win and sometimes you learn," and that's exactly what I experienced. People will always be people. Some will surprise you and some will disappoint you.

Within the real estate team, I saw firsthand how greed set in for some teammates, and how the grass began to look greener on the other side. Most people forget who cultivated, planted, watered, fertilized, and cut the grass for a decade before they saw the green, healthy, beautiful, and mature results. I had two buyer's agents leave the team and become my competitors by joining another real estate firm. They thought they could do what I did and make more money. I can honestly say that time will always tell the best story. Never say you have finished a book until you read the final chapter.

We went from a team of five to a team of three, and we took our businesses to the highest level. Our game plan was to get prospects in, sign them up as clients, find them a house, and close eight deals a month. This was a big goal, and we expected even bigger results. After all, we were the Results Partners.

As a team, we experienced the ultimate high in production, selling more than 80 homes each year. For perspective, the average agent sold 12 homes a year. I thought this was a good way to become wealthy. Buying, selling, and investing in making your dreams come true. I got laser-focused and started reading lots of real estate books, which helped me to establish and implement systems to set me up for my best year ever, which was just around the corner. Team work makes the dream work!

In 2006, our team wrote 117 contracts and closed 113 deals in one single year. This is the reason I love real estate. It will never go out of style, because people will always need a roof over their heads. I know that they will either rent or they will own, but either way, if hired as their realtor, I would have an opportunity to be on the winning team. During this period, my husband and I, along with another business partner, purchased over 70 homes in a six-year span. We personally were blessed to have bought, rehabbed, rented, and managed 39 rental properties, while we continued to flip the others. From 1973-2014, we had

> *Team work makes the dream work!*

accumulated a total of 155 personal properties We give all Glory to God.

~ Client Appreciation ~

There is an old saying, "Remember the bridges that brought you over, and never burn them." This is definitely a true statement for me. I embrace this concept and know that hard work alone was not solely responsible for my success as a realtor. Favor, purpose, always trying to do the right thing, and doing right by people are all knitted and woven together to make the pieces of the puzzle fit.

In real estate prospecting, we classify groups of people as a Cold or Warm market prospects. I can testify that giving back, showing appreciation, and building relationships, were, and still are, the key to growing my warm market. This has been the anchor for my continued high productivity.

I've always loved giving back, and thought, "What better way to give back to my clients, than to host a big party with lots of prizes?" We hosted our first Client Appreciation Celebration in 1990. This idea was, and still is, all about saying thank you to the people who chose to do business with us. Our first event was standing room only. It was a huge success, and I knew then and there that I needed a much bigger venue, since my goal was to do bigger business.

My annual client appreciation events were always well attended and thoroughly enjoyed by all. The events varied from picnics in the park, to large house parties, to formal affairs in December, to casual outings by the lake in late summer. These are the perfect settings to get together, network, catch up, and celebrate the past year's production. The events are always full of prizes and giveaways to those loyal clients who continue to send referrals year after year and help keep my business moving in the right direction. Warm market business is a real blessing. You don't have to reintroduce yourself quite so much. You just have to continue creating raving fans, one generation after the other.

I was, and still am, the exclusive realtor who gives back continuously to clients by hosting the ultimate Client Appreciation Celebration. There is always great food, music, entertainment, and tons of prizes all for my past clients. I love referrals, and my clients continue to send them. In fact, they are happy and eager to send referrals, because they look forward to qualifying for the VIP Grand Prize contest, where cash prizes, destination trips, and gifts are given away each year. We created lots of games to give away the prizes. Some big hits were "Let's Make a Deal", "Who

Wants to Be a Millionaire", and lots of trivia about my real estate career. However, their favorite game is getting 30 seconds in the money machine and having the opportunity to grab up to $2,000 in cash. My clients still rave about our VIP Grand Prize games. The Client Appreciation Celebration is a 20 plus year tradition and I love hosting it.

~The Mid East Experience~

In 2006, I got a call from a young man who I had never met. He called me with a direct request from his very ill mother who I had also never met. The request was so strange that I asked the son to meet me at my lawyer's office for a legal ear on what they were proposing. Here are two people I didn't know wanting me to buy a property. I will never forget this property. Mainly because it was in a rural part Richland County where we would have never considered investing in real estate.

The woman asked her son to call me to buy their property because she was in a nursing home and she was in financial trouble. She had been ordered to sell the house in order to pay her bills and handle a couple of other matters. She really needed the cash from the sale of this home. After hearing about her situation from her son, my heart was touched. Her son told me that she said, "Though I've never met Mrs. Nancy Johnson, I was at a garage sale somewhere and heard her name. I want her to buy my house so that I can stay in this nursing home."

Though we typically did not invest in properties in this part of town, we decided to buy the property. The house was on Mid East Road in Eastover, SC. It had a lot of potential but also needed some repairs. We decided to fix it up and sell the home. As it turned out, a couple from Florida looked at the home and were more interested in renting the property versus buying it. We made the decision to rent the home out to them. Four months later, in the middle of winter, they decided that the home was too much for them to handle. They asked to opt out of their lease. We graciously allowed them to break the lease. A few days later, the couple was in the process of moving out of the house. Most of the furniture was gone and they were doing laundry drying their area rugs in the dryer. The dryer caught on fire! Before they knew it, the entire house was up in flames and was a total loss. We thank God that nobody was hurt. We were also extremely thankful that our wisdom paid off. When we purchased the home, we made sure we carried good insurance. This allowed the house to be completely replaced.

  Approximately a year or so later, one of the original owner's family members called and left a message. The lady that we purchased the property from had passed away. They didn't remember to inform me that she passed but they called to thank me for buying the house. The woman's last days were her best days. She was able to use the money that she made from our purchase of the home to live her last days in comfort.

We were a blessing to her and she was a blessing to us. In the end, this home on Mid East netted us nearly $100,000 in the end. The lesson for me is when you help someone in need out of the goodness of your heart, you'll be rewarded for your goodness. To paraphrase the good book, with clean hands and a pure heart favor will abound.

~ Recession – Regroup – Rebound - Recover ~

Before the Great Recession, this country girl was flying high in the good years. I was doing well in real estate. The market was thriving and so was my business. In 2007, I had increased my annual income ten-fold from where it was when I started in 1987. We had a lot of success over this time period. I also had achieved many accolades. I was the first African American woman in the Four Million Dollar Club of the Greater Columbia Board of Realtors. I also closed six transactions in one day and sold eleven homes in one month. My production was strong, and I became the number one agent in the southeast United States with buyer-controlled transactions and I have the trophy to prove it.

When you're a hardworking country girl with no wealthy role model in your circle, it can cause your vision to be nearsighted. I thought doubling my Blue Cross income was a big deal. I was content with that goal. In hindsight, I was really selling myself short. I should have known I could have been even more successful. I didn't realize that the sky was the limit, and that more could have been accomplished.

Then along came the Great Recession. The banks tightened up lending requirements and very few people could qualify to buy a home. I didn't have many buyers anyway. There were fewer people buying during this time because of fear and uncertainty. Many people were losing their jobs, and others were losing their homes to foreclosure. My business suffered dramatically. In my best year before the recession, I sold 113 homes. One year during the recession, I sold only 29 homes. That was a 75% loss in production and income.

The length of the recession had me gasping for breath. It lasted for seven years. I felt stifled and struggled for a way to be optimistic that things would soon get back to normal. The media's continued bashing, and the constant reminder of the bleak economic forecast had me constantly asking myself, "When will this end?" I wondered how much more could the real estate market bear? Seven years of a recession was hard. I saw the best of the best years in my career between 2003 and 2009, and now I was experiencing the worst years in my real estate career. It was like riding on the highest roller coaster ever. I had started up high, and now I was down way low.

Up to this point, deals were seemingly falling into our laps like manna from the sky. But during the recession, our personal finances also took a big hit. We thought we had made all the right decisions. We had great credit, built up a hefty savings, and had little debt, except for the mortgages on the 39 properties that we had accumulated over the years. Our net worth was over a million dollars. We had made it far from where we started; living in a small wooden home, with outdoor toilets, and no heating or air. We were now supposed to be in a better place, and we were to an extent, before this twister of a recession came and tore up the economy, my business, and our finances.

The recession threw us a curveball, more like a monkey wrench, which applied financial pressure similar to a pressure cooker. The type of pressure that bursts pipes. The pressure got tighter and tighter for what seemed like a lifetime. To recover, I had to use my faith as my anchor. I knew somewhere in the back of my mind that God didn't bring me this far to leave me now. I would quote the scripture, "To whom much is given, much is required." Business was now slow, and money was tight for most people in and out of my circle.

How do you stay encouraged and stay positive when everything you see and hear says that America is falling apart? There were a lot of agents that gave up on real estate during the recession. It was very hard to keep your head in the game when you were losing it all. I had a lot on the table, and I was determined to recover it all, come hell or high water.

I decided to keep showing up to the office every day. I prospected everywhere for buyers. I was always working to find another real estate deal and even to find another real estate niche. I had to do something. I had to find a new creative way to keep moving. I was too close to retirement, so I couldn't give up. I had to reach beyond what I saw with the natural eye and keeping my eyes beyond the hills where my help comes from. I had to dig deep and do what champions do when they get knocked down. They look up and then they get up, by pulling on their inner strength to fight another round. Champions don't stay down for the count.

Purpose, passion, and destiny kicked in. I had to sit back and really think about that. The simple fact was that even though unemployment, bankruptcy, foreclosures, short sales, and business shutdowns were at an all-time high, and the stock market was at an all-time low, there were still clients to serve. I knew that people still needed to either rent or buy, because they would still need a place to live, in spite of difficult times.

I had to implement the practice of self-talk. I had to remind myself not to take this struggle personally, because the truth was that this gorilla called "The Recession" had a wide net of devastation to all. I thought, "And this too shall pass." About four years into the recession, after walking around with my tail tucked between my legs, I decided to roll up my sleeves, and with new determination, declared that I was too close to retirement not to regroup and recover it all.

I got my second wind, took off my flip flops, put on my running shoes, and decided to take advantage of my margin, and supplement my real estate income. Our rental homes were paying off greatly, and they were a great supplemental income to us during this severe financial crisis. Very few of our tenants had experienced job losses, and that was a blessing. Many were on Section 8, a rental housing supplemental program, and we could count on their rent being on time each month.

Another big factor for us personally, was that I heeded some wise advice given to me by my favorite uncle, C.J. He was a real savvy businessman, and family man, with only a fourth-grade education. He taught his children, and those who were around him, not to spend everything that came through their hands. I remembered his lessons about banking potatoes and applied it to my life. It was such an amazing but simple concept—when you get money, don't spend everything you make. Save some for a rainy day because there could be bad times ahead.

Throughout my whole life, this wisdom stuck with me, as I used my God-given hands to manage what we had, so that we could survive in the recession. Using this wisdom, we rebuilt our broken pieces. We managed to keep our household and most of our investments afloat. Truth be told, we lost some things along the way, but I had to remember that it wasn't personal. It was the gorilla called recession, and although he wasn't looking for me by name, he was just as determined to devour anybody in his sight.

~ Speak Over yourself ~

What goes up must come down. And boy did the Big Gorilla come down. From 2010-2013, the recession caused me to shut down, or should I say, postpone my annual Client Appreciation Celebration during those years. I was grateful for the little bit of business that I had, but the truth was, my world was spinning out of control. I had gone from being number one and closing eight to ten deals per month, to hardly closing one or two deals per month. I wouldn't wish this gorilla on anyone's back ever again.

It had been said that the financial recession we lived through was only second to the Great Depression, which lasted three times as long. I had to keep telling myself, "This recession is not personal. Everybody is losing stuff." All across the world, people were suffering, and were probably worse off than my family was.

Due to the recession, I had to cut my staff, and I was rolling solo. I went from having a team of five members down to just me, myself, and I. I didn't even have an assistant anymore. I had to learn how to shift, refocus, compartmentalize, and prioritize. I was thinking to myself, "Some extra money would sure look good in our account right about now." I even began to supplement my income by helping my daughter with her network marketing business. I had limited options and resources. Not only was I a realtor whose business was suffering due to the recession, but I was also a seasoned investor who couldn't buy rental property because the banks froze our credit lines. My nest egg and plans for early retirement primarily revolved around real estate that I owned, which had now lost value and equity. I literally had to start over, and delay my retirement plans to recover the bulk of money that was lost.

I now had to pull myself up by the bootstraps and go to work, just like on the farm. The impact of the recession was very deep, and the recovery was slow. I prayed more than ever for business to come my way. It took a toll on my family, my health, and my finances. But my belief in God, spiritual strength, and faith never wavered. I just kept speaking favor over my life, working my business, and having bounce-back faith. My husband and children always believed in my real estate business and supported me every step of the way.

> *My belief in God, spiritual strength, and faith never wavered.*

There wasn't anything that I did, or did not do, that caused havoc on my business. I had to console myself by repeatedly chanting, "This too shall pass...This too shall pass..." There were many days when I wanted to hide, and many days I cried, because I didn't want people to know how the recession had broken me.

Then I reflected on how far I had come in my life. I had to remember that I started my life as a poor country girl, who used to hide in the back of a pickup truck after missing a day of school to go pick cotton. Now I was selling and buying homes that a poor country girl could never even dream of walking in, much less living in. I'm no longer hiding, but instead, putting my face and phone number on billboards, and blasting my number for people to call.

Now, it is my business to open doors for you! My pastor said it best when he said, "Some people develop historical amnesia, and they forget who brought them over and through the Jordan River. But no matter where you end up, tell God thank you!"

Slowly, things began to turn around on the real estate front. President Barack Obama rolled out the "Cash for Clunkers" program, and also rolled out a down-payment assistance program, which provided prospective home buyers with $5,000 to $7,000 in down-payment funds to purchase new homes. This program lasted for a couple of years, and it helped get the market moving in the right direction. The down-payment assistance program was so effective that it was extended for a longer period of time. Though this was a good indicator that things were getting better, I knew things were still not what I would call back to normal, and we were not out of the woods yet.

I kept hope alive, and we did finally begin to gain ground again. "Keep hope alive...Keep hope alive" became my mantra for that season. In 2013-2014, I saw a light at the end of the tunnel.

> *Little did I know that there was a blessing in the pressing!*

Although it was dim, it was visible, and I was optimistic, believing that things would get better, and return to normal.

Little did I know that there was a blessing in my pressing forward. And it happened right on time. My production was coming back. The referrals were slow, and one-third of my business, which was working with investors, was not yet picking up. During the recession investors were not able to get financing as easily as they were before. Banks were not lending like they used to, so my investors had to seek out hard money lenders, which had less than favorable financing terms. As a result, down-payments for investors doubled, and tripled. So now I thought, "Where do I turn to fill the void of my investor-projected income?" This was a big dilemma, as with no investors investing, I had a big void to fill.

I needed to find a niche that worked for me, and one that worked quickly. I began to ask myself the following questions:

- *What other niches of real estate can I utilize for income?*
- *How can I do what I do on a larger scale than one-on-one with the client?*
- *What skills, other than real estate, can I employ as a substitute?*
- *What am I good at?*
- *What are my gifts?*

I determined that I love real estate and would do it whether I got paid or not. I concluded that I could teach, coach, put on seminars, do joint ventures with other investors, host boot camps, manage properties, or show others how to use real estate as a wealth vehicle. I declared that I could do all these things to live in the margin. Tough times will cause you to become resourceful.

I decided to increase my social media marketing, and expand my method of networking, to help me bounce back. I no longer had a team, or two assistants. That became a thing of the past. As they say in real estate and other businesses, if you do not have an assistant, then you are the assistant. This was a challenging time, which called for an activation of faith, extraordinary strength, endurance, perseverance, and learning new things.

And boy, did I have to learn a lot. I was what you called old school. I was a yellow pad writing, high-touch, low-tech agent. I was not computer-savvy, nor was I into advanced technology. I had to learn how to use a computer, respond to emails, use a scanner, and print property sheets. I also had to improve upon my organizational skills and prioritizing techniques. While on my learning journey, I also resorted back to prospecting for business the old-fashioned way, which was by word-of-mouth.

What do you do when you're going through tough times, and there seems to be nothing else you can do? All you can do is stand. I showed up every day, even when the phones weren't ringing. There were only a few contracts, and closings were down to a trickle. But when you love and believe in what you do, you will find a way to win, because you will not quit. I read a book that taught me how to win in the margin and leave nothing on the table. I learned that when you use all your gifts, they will make room for you. I had the will to win.

~ When the Glory Comes: Real Estate Niche ~

I mentioned that working with investors became a third of my business before the recession. Investors are people who buy real estate to flip for a profit, or they rent property to others for a profit. When I first started working with investors, I would help them find properties through the Multiple Listing Service (MLS). Over time, I learned there were other ways to find investment property. The chief way most investors purchased properties were through the county court system at the Master of Equity sales. The Master of Equity Sale is how the county disposes of bank foreclosed properties.

I began to attend the Master-in-Equity sales, watching how they work, and strategizing how I could best get into the game of buying foreclosed properties. The bidding at the Master-in-Equity sales is fast and furious, and you had better do your homework before bidding on or buying a property. In my opinion, it is one of the riskiest ways to buy real estate, but also, one of the most profitable.

Here's how it goes. A local newspaper will list all the properties that will be up for auction on the first Monday of the month at noon. The process is so risky, because there are some homes that are still occupied. Therefore, you cannot access them to check out their condition before buying them. Many homes at these sales are purchased sight unseen. Some of the homes are boarded up, or plagued with multiple mortgages, unpaid property taxes, liens, etc. This is why it's so important to go to the courthouse, do your due diligence, and thoroughly investigate each property individually before the sale date.

On the day of the sale, you arrive, sit and wait until the property that you are interested in is called, and then you get ready to bid. The bidding war begins with the attorney for the lienholder starting the bid. You have to be awake, alert, and speak fast, or you will get left in the dust, and miss the opportunity to buy the property you were intending to bid on.

The room is usually pretty full, with approximately 50-75 people in attendance. Some of the people there were the homeowners who are unfortunately losing their homes. However, most folks are just there to watch. There are about 10-12 people who actually participate in the auction, who aggressively bid, and who end up buying one or more homes in this process. Most of the bidders are investors like me who are looking to successful purchase a property or two.

Purchasing properties this way became a game-changer for me, and I didn't even realize it. It wasn't until I started writing this book that I realized the implications and impact of being in the financial position I was in at that time. You had to be in a position to pay cash for the homes you were bidding on. Just think, 40 years prior, I had been a poor, black, cotton-picking country girl with nothing to show for it, but now I was sitting in a courtroom amongst financially-savvy investors, competing and purchasing real estate deals to create wealth. God did promise that He would make me the head and not the tail.

I can vividly remember sitting in the courtroom one day, and bidding on properties fast and furiously. Bank of America and Citibank were unloading their large inventory of homes in Richland County, South Carolina. Before I knew it, I had accumulated up to six properties in one single day. I was having success bidding in a sea of shark tank real estate investors. I kept hearing the song, "This Place" by Tamela Mann playing in my head. Just as the song states, "I never thought I'd be in this place!" God showed me during this experience that He allowed me to be the only woman, and the only African-American investor, at the Master-in-Equity sales, that was bidding on and buying real estate. This was a different table that I had imagined. God had made room for me at THIS table, and I was ecstatic.

Many people had lost things during the recession. We lost homes during that time. Our credit was shot too. It was rough, tough and depressing, but it was also a great time for those investors who were financially positioned to take advantage of the abundance of real estate that other individuals had lost. My uncle C.J.'s principle of banking sweet potatoes served us well during this time. For those who were financially prepared, it was a great time to buy properties with cash at bargain-basement prices, rent properties, or hold properties for future equity build-up. It was time to take the lemons of the recession and make lemonade.

There were so many valuable lessons I learned during the recession. One of those was recognizing the true value of real estate. It proved to be a great option when it came to investing because there is always a demand. Though there were so many foreclosures, misfortunes, and job losses during the recession, people always needed a place to live, whether they needed to rent it, own it, or downsize to a smaller house, there was always a demand.

The exposure to the Master-in-Equity sales was one of the most valuable experiences in my entire real estate career. I can honestly say there were things I didn't know, but I learned them quickly. It is a lesson of what is possible in your life. I went from the cotton field to the capital city, and I measured up.

The story of going from growing up dirt poor, no indoor plumbing, reading and doing homework by my kerosene lamp light, sleeping two to three deep in one single bed, or on a cot to stay warm and survive, to being able to live in a nice house, in a nice community, drive my own nice car, and be financially comfortable, still blows my mind. God has been better than good to me!

> *I went from the cotton field to the capital city, and I measured up*

~A Big Leap of Faith~

Up until the year 2001, we primarily only invested in residential property. I was familiar with commercial real estate, but we never really invested in commercial property. In 2001, we started to notice the explosive growth happening in our community of Northeast Columbia. There were lots of families and businesses moving into the area. For several years, I struggled to find the perfect place to host my annual Client Appreciation Celebration. There wasn't really a good conference center to host weddings or reception events either. So, we decided to take a leap of faith and purchase two acres of prime property for $150,000. We had plans to build our own one-stop-shop conference center. The property was located at Clemson Road and I-20 East which was a prime location for almost any business that wanted to be noticed. Plus, it was on a desirable frontage road. I never thought of paying $75,000 an acre. I definitely never imagined paying that for a piece of raw land.

Shortly after purchasing the land, our plans changed. Ronnie began to have a few health issues, so we decided to not build the one-stop-shop conference center. We decided to hold on to the property even though we no longer had an immediate use for it. We knew to have two acres of land on a frontage road in the fastest-growing part of town was going to pay off one day, and it did. These two acres became one of the best investments we ever made.

A year after we purchased it, the property went up in value. As fate would have it, someone else had a vision in mind for the two acres that we owned. Another business owner was building on the property adjacent to ours but needed a portion of our two acres to complete their project. They offered us almost triple what we purchased it for just two years prior. We did absolutely nothing to improve the land which is what made this deal even sweeter. We knew they wanted the land badly and may have been willing to pay any price to get it. We could have played hardball to max out our profit on this deal. However, we didn't do that. While the deal was in negotiations, I was in Atlanta, Georgia at a *Woman, Thou Are Loosed* conference hosted by Bishop T.D. Jakes. I was there listening for God's voice in all of my life decisions. The Lord spoke to me and said, "Do what is fair." Instead of pushing for a higher price, we named our fair price and they agreed to the deal. Two years after taking a leap of faith, commercial real estate paid big dividends.

> *Two years after taking a leap of faith, commercial real estate paid big dividends.*

~ Paradise Was Part of The Journey ~

My real estate career has had more highs than lows. In fact, the only period of low production I remember was during the recession. For the first 24 years of my real estate career, I experienced exponential growth each year. I was truly blessed and favored with an awesome real estate career. I have always been a team player, and I love to win, but I also get joy from helping others and seeing them excel at whatever they do in life. My goals and thoughts for real estate production were no exception. If you are a part of my team, just know I play big, aim high, and want everyone who contributes to enjoy the ride.

For four consecutive years, I treated my entire team, the Results Partners, to an all-expense paid four-day trip, as a token of my appreciation for our achievements. I took them to Paradise Island, Bahamas!

The annual trip was exciting, fun, good for the team morale, and something we always looked forward to. Some would say, "Wow! Wasn't that expensive?" my answer was no. My rationale was that the trip was funded by collectively hitting our numbers, reaching our aggressive goals, and selling more than we did the previous year. I would set aside the commission from two to three deals to pay for it. I budgeted accordingly, and this worked out well for all the teammates and their spouses. These trips were designed for resting and relaxation. We stayed at an exclusive, all-inclusive resort on Paradise Island, which ultimately made for better production, and a way to create lots of fun and lasting memories. I treasure those trips and have never heard of any agent in my market doing the same thing for their team.

~ The People on My Journey ~

--I'm pinching pennies but I'm buying this house--

My client was a veteran, and had limited funds, however, I saw firsthand what "breaking the bank" was about. He had scraped up what he had and came up with $260 in coins to close on his new home. The attorney said, "Man, it's 5 o'clock! What am I supposed to do with all this change?"

We closed the transaction and he walked away with the keys to his new home. The last I heard, he is still in the same home after purchasing it over 25 years ago.

--Moe and Roy--

I really loved these two. My husband, daughter, and staff call me "The Yellow Pad Queen", because anything I hear, I scribble it down on a yellow pad. And I am notorious for issuing out daily to-do lists, but I believe that I had met my match in Moe and Roy. Moe and Roy had me beat with writing down everything.

These older investors were retired. One was a fireman, and they allowed me to list a few of their properties, even though I was a new agent without much experience. They also believed in me, and owner-financed about five of our first rental properties. I will always remember these two guys.

They both drove older-model rundown trucks and dressed in coveralls. One chewed tobacco, and one carried the notepad as their computer to keep tabs on what came in and what went out. They knew down to the penny who owed them and when it was due. They were very nice guys, and they knew how to create wealth in real estate, and that's what I valued most.

Lesson learned—never judge a person by the coveralls they wear. Some people see business before race.

--*The Skyscrapers*--

My New York wealth builders' purchases produced nine transactions with me. In 1989, I met a couple who made all the right financial moves, and who were returning South. They both had great jobs. One was an accountant, and the other worked with the postal service. They had sold an apartment building in New York, and relocated to Columbia, South Carolina to continue working and raising their two young daughters. This couple was also originally from one of the poorest counties in South Carolina.

The big takeaway for investors is knowing the market and learning that you can create wealth anywhere with real estate. Over the years, we developed a great relationship. I sold them nine properties. I took pleasure in playing a role in them achieving the "Ultimate Investor's Dream", which was paying off all nine properties in 20 years and owning them free and clear. Now that's "Making House Money"!

--*Follow the doctor's orders*--

One day I received an interesting call from a person who was interested in one of my listings. He was a doctor from out of town, and he wanted to place a cash offer on a townhouse that he had never laid his eyes on. It was a 3 bedroom, 1 ½ bath townhome that needed about $1,500 in minor repairs.

I followed his orders, signed him up, wrote the contract, got the offer accepted, and it closed 15 days later while I was on vacation. And this one gets better!

While I was checking on the property, the sister of the tenant next door was visiting, and wanted to know if it was for rent. I exclaimed, "Of course!" We proceeded to negotiate, and I leased the apartment to her for $700 per month, and the rest is history.

What a wise investment. If he would have let his money sit in the bank, he wouldn't have earned much interest. But by making this wise investment, my client generated $700 in passive income per month. To this day, I have only seen a photo of this client, because my assistant attended the closing in my absence. Now this is an example of making money while you sleep, travel, and relax.

This one was quick, painless, and easy money for me. And although it was a small deal for me, I was overjoyed because it was a big deal for my client.

--Church Place and Melrose Heights--

These are two neighborhoods that struggled at one time. The City of Columbia sought to revitalize these communities and asked me to help. Some of our clients in these neighborhoods were uneducated, homeless, and may have never owned any property except for this opportunity. Owning a house wasn't even on their bucket list. To this day, both neighborhoods still look good, and have had only a few turnovers. I was blessed to be one of their exclusive marketing agents and sold nearly all of them myself.

A local church was the main anchor, as well as several retired faculty members from a nearby historically black college. This particular church was known for its great soul food dinners, however, the deterioration of the location scared off many potential customers. The city's vision was to clean up, fix up, or sell the surrounding real estate. They sold the idea to three local churches, and they ended up building homes for the seniors of their congregations.

What an amazing transformation. Instead of being a neighborhood full of abandoned and slum apartments, shotgun and boarded up wooden homes, this area was now full of nice and new 3-bedroom, 2-bathroom brick homes. The buyers only had to pay a $500 down-payment, and their mortgage payments were only $500 per month! This neighborhood was in an ideal location in downtown Columbia, right on the bus line, and near hospitals and clinics. Praise God for allowing me to be a part of something this great, and for allowing me to witness such an amazing transformation of two communities.

--I Know There's More...--

I met this young mother around 1982, shortly after attending church with a co-worker in Columbia. She had been through life's ups and downs and was recently divorced with two daughters to raise. The amazing thing about my friend, who became a solid, seasoned investor, is that she never lost faith. She would always say, "Nancy, I know there's more to life. I trust God to take care of me and the girls!"

Over a period of time, we talked, set goals, shared our ideas, and now this single mom owns seven or eight properties.

Like with her faith, she never wavered. She pursued and received more.

--A Place to Worship--

I always understood that real estate would never go out of style. There will always be a demand for real estate. Whether it's a place to eat, be entertained or shop until you drop, there will always be a demand for real estate. There is also a need for real estate for people of faith who want to worship together.

During my career I have helped multiple religious organizations with their needs. Whether it's acquiring land to build, building a church, or renovating a church, I have been there.

It's been an honor to be a part of locating, negotiating and closing transactions for the following churches in Columbia, SC: Rehoboth United; Northeast Bible Way Temple now known as Open Door Ministries; North Point Community Church; Bible Way Church of

Atlas Road; Hope Lutheran Church, The Brook, and Kingdom Vision Church.

~ The No Excuse Zone ~

I could have allowed all the excuses in the world to come into my head and force me to give in to the mindset of accepting average as the norm. But I'm so glad that I didn't settle when I supposedly hit the fake glass ceiling in corporate America after 19 years of service. I would have never been able to experience my real passion, real estate.

> *Excuses don't excuse.*

I remember an English teacher saying, "Excuses don't excuse," and I honestly believe that to be true. Would've, could've, and should've is like being hungry with a mouth full of food, and not putting forth any effort to chew it. You will never solve the hunger problem that way.

No matter where you're born, or what you go through, I've learned that excuses don't churn milk into butter. Wood sitting in the fireplace will never ignite itself. In life, you have to do something if you want to be somebody and have something. Your belief has to be stronger than your excuses. My life could have crumbled many times through dangers seen and unseen, but I've never been a person full of excuses.

> *Your belief has to be stronger than your excuses.*

I was born to a single mother, I had no fatherly love, and we were barely getting by. We were "poor and poor some more". Even during those times, I always had hope and optimism. I remember days I needed five cents for personal items and couldn't find a nickel anywhere...no excuses. I still went to school, sat

> *Excuses don't excuse or exclude you from the ups and downs of life.*

tall, and did my best. If I had no transportation to the public library to get a book that the school didn't have, I walked miles to get the book and picked up two good ones while I was there...no excuses. Not having a college degree could have slowed my progress in the corporate world...no excuses. Hitting the glass ceiling, being pushed too hard...no excuses. They meant it for evil, but it worked for my good. I was living then, and I'm still living now in the "No Excuse Zone."

Some said if you marry too young, it won't last. Well, some marriages do, and some don't. Those who don't complain and press through the valleys to make it to the mountaintop seldom make excuses. Why? Because excuses don't excuse or exclude you from the ups and downs of life. Excuses are weak and fearful.

To all who are reading this book, just know that when you take a licking, keep on ticking. When you have lemons, make lemonade. When you are taking action you are not making excuses. It works if you are willing to work it like you want it. I wanted it bad and I seldom made excuses for why I couldn't do something. Therefore, I have been blessed to do a bunch of things! Isn't God good?

~ Conclusion ~

Have you ever found yourself in a place where you least expected to be? Sometimes I have to pinch myself and wonder how I got over. The Lord has been better than good to me. He is my anchor, my bridge, and the wind beneath my wings. I have been places, sat in the presence of people, and knew at those times that my steps were set up by the Almighty God.

In my insurance career, I reached the glass ceiling because I didn't have a college degree. I'd like to say I got pushed out of a place where I could not climb higher, and landed in real estate, and that's where God showed me His favor, and like an eagle, I soared higher than ever imagined. God's favor is nothing but the truth! All my help comes from above. It was a setup and I'm glad about it. Real estate has been good to me and for me. I blazed many trails, and my hope is that those who read this book fully appreciate and understand my journey, and why I chose to share it. I accomplished, set, and broke many records with the favor of God, and a lot of hard work.

One thing about being poor, is that when you do not have some of the finer things in life, you can appreciate and acknowledge the differences once you've received them. A poor mindset will not allow your potential to develop. There was never a time in my life when I was convinced that I would not, or could not, make it, be successful, or have a good life. I always had strong beliefs, and an even stronger determination to make it out of the poorest of conditions. Whatever I did, my Aunt Honey always encouraged me, and told me that I had to be twice as good to get half as far. All of my elders, and the people in my village taught me manners. They would say, "Manners would carry you where money won't." They were so right. Something deep inside of me always says if it's worth doing, give it all you've got. You have to be passionate and strive to rise to the top.

I could have found many reasons to bury my potential, and to just be ordinary. However, making excuses was never an option for me...not in school, not at work, not at whatever I pursued. Making excuses never leads to greatness or extraordinary results. If there was an opportunity of interest, I took it on like I owned it!

> *Manners will carry you where money won't.*

Whether the path was easy or challenging, I was all-in and dripping with passion to see it through. In my mind, controlling my real estate destiny was the power I needed to possess, so that I did not get sucked into the poor mentality of the environment I was raised in. I had made up my mind that I was going to be a true, consummate, real estate professional, and an extraordinary realtor with no excuses. Even though I didn't have a role model in the real estate industry, nor a success model to guide me on this real estate journey, my childhood and upbringing had prepared me for this. This was somewhat of a familiar place for me, and my passion and drive gave me the vision to become the first role model in my industry to create the Road Map to Real Estate and Investment Success for those who enter this profession after me.

I frequently tell my story of living in a poor community, being shifted between various family members' houses, with limited to no means, using an outhouse as our restroom, and not having central heat or air conditioning. I tell that story, not so people can feel sorry for me, but to show them that excuses don't excuse them from trying. I could have made a million and one excuses as to why I should quit or not rise to the occasion and become a leader, but I chose not to. God delivered me from a place of lack to a place of abundance. Even during the recession, He kept me, and kept blessing me and my family as we moved from the cotton fields and the dirt roads, from a one-bedroom house to the big house and gave us plenty of investment homes too.

My husband and I worked extremely hard, and always had a passion to create wealth. We had absolutely no one to depend on financially but each other. There were no silver spoons in our lineage. I once heard someone define POOR as:

P—Passing

O—Over

O—Opportunity

R—Repeatedly

This wasn't a definition that I was going to let shape nor define my life. Instead, I choose to create, chase, and seize opportunity.

Being full of gifts, talent, and opportunities to create a better lifestyle is where passion can drive you from the cotton field to the places you never dreamed possible. I hope and pray everyone reading this book will be inspired, whether now or later, to never allow your past to determine your future. With Christ on your side, anything is possible.

~ About the Author ~

Nancy E. Johnson has made it her business to open doors for thousands of people in the real estate industry. Her commitment, authenticity, and integrity have made her one of the most successful real estate agents and investors in South Carolina's history. In a career that spans three decades, Nancy has been involved in helping thousands of families achieve the American Dream of homeownership.

Starting her career in the health insurance industry, Nancy has always been focused on helping and serving people. From her first day in 1969 as a file clerk at Blue Cross & Blue Shield, to ultimately serving as the manager of the Major Medical division with 64 employees reporting to her, Nancy has been a leader in business for many years. Her success in the company was unprecedented, receiving 15 promotions over a 19-year career, and ultimately becoming the second African-American supervisor, and the second African-American woman to reach the position of manager in the company. As a woman in corporate America, Nancy faced her challenges as well. She was barred from being promoted to the director of her department, because she lacked a college degree. After facing this glass ceiling in corporate America, Nancy refused to be held back by the artificial barrier of a college degree. She quit her corporate job in health insurance, became a full-time real estate entrepreneur, and has not looked back.

In 1986, Nancy became the first African-American realtor to be hired by Gallup and Associates, and Coldwell Banker Tom Jenkins Realty. Nancy used her experience in business to hone her skills in customer service and relationship development. Nancy ate, slept, and breathed real estate for her first ten years in the business. Her commitment to her craft of opening doors for new home buyers in Columbia, South Carolina, allowed her to achieve an amazing milestone of becoming the only African-American in the history of the Columbia Board of Realtors to reach the Four Million Dollar Club in a single year. It was at this point in her professional career that Nancy began to expand her operations beyond sole-proprietorship. She was one of the first realtors in Columbia to hire an assistant, and ultimately grew her staff to a team of five.

Nancy and her husband have managed to purchase many properties of their own by implementing strategies she mastered while helping friends, family, church members, and former co-workers buy their first homes. By helping thousands of others to succeed at homeownership, Nancy developed her own unique real estate investment strategy she now calls "Making House Money ™". As a real estate investor, Nancy has used her proven system to achieve astonishing results.

In Nancy's 33-year career as a real estate professional, she has worked with all types of clients, from first-time homebuyers to seasoned real estate investors. Nancy lives by her motto, "It is my business to open doors for you". It is this approach to serving her customers and clients, which allowed her to show nearly 2,300 individuals how to transition from renters to homeowners or investors. Through her boot camps, seminars, workshops, and real estate coaching programs, she provides participants with the tips, tools, and insight to become successful in real estate in less than 18 months.

Nancy has become one of the nation's premier real estate experts and has been featured in articles in *Agent & Broker* magazine and has written articles for *How We Live* magazine. She has served as a keynote speaker for conferences, forums, and commencement ceremonies in multiple states. She has also been a regular guest on multiple radio talk shows.

Nancy is currently a Broker-Agent at ERA Wilder Realty and has been involved in thousands of real estate transactions and acquisitions. She resides in Columbia, South Carolina with her husband of 51 years, Ronnie Johnson.

Connect with Nancy

Facebook: @nancyejohnsonteam

Instagram: @nancyopensdoors

LinkedIn: linkedin.com/in/nancy-johnson-ab785944

Website: https://www.NancyOpensDoors.com

Made in the USA
Middletown, DE
04 October 2023